The Prayer Of Jabez in The Market Place Journal

Welcome! Congratulations on getting your copy of the "The Prayer of Jabez in the Marketplace Journal". The purpose of the journal is to help you make The Prayer of Jabez personal and intentional. This journal is best used in conjunction with the book "The Prayer of Jabez in the Market Place" but it can be used independently without it. The journal is broken into five sections and aligns with the exercises in the book in more detail.

Word of The Day

In order to be intentional and making it personal we have to attach the real meaning of words. Words have power and when used in the correct context can be enlightening. In this section you will have 10 words provide and you will add 20 more words that partian to your business.

Practice Gratitude

Positive energy creates positive energy. One of the key ways to experiencing peace and joy in your life is to practice gratitude. This section helps you to practice gratitude everyday even in those difficult times when finding things to be thankful for can be hard.

Prayers

In this section, you will pray The Prayer of Jabez and develop your prayers. You will also have specific activities in this section to develop prayers and vows that are intentioal, personal and full of power.

Journal Entry

This section helps you identify and confront what you are truly looking for. You will take a deep dive into where you want your business to be extended to. This section assist in bringing clarity to how you want to enlarge your territory.

Visualize what you want

In this section you will create a vision and action plan for the woman you want to be. Your plans will assist you with identifying your purpose, visualizing what you want, setting goals, defining your why, and the actions require to manifest your vision.

The Prayer of Jabez

Jabez cried out to the God of Israel, "Oh, that you would bless me and enlarge my territory! Let your hand be with me, and keep me from harm so that I will be free from pain." And God granted his request.

1 Chronicles 4:10 NIV

Word of the Day

Alignment
a state of agreement or cooperation among persons, groups, nations, etc., with a common cause or viewpoint.

The Prayer of Jabez

Make It Personal & Intentional

_____ cried out to the God of Israel, "Oh, that you would bless me and enlarge my_____ _____! Let your hand be with me, and keep me from harm so that I will be free from pain." And God granted his request.

1 Chronicles 4:10 NIV

My Daily Journal

DAY:

Today, I accomplished :

_____
_____
_____
_____
_____

My Goals For Tomorrow:

_____
_____
_____
_____

MyThoughts:

_____
_____
_____
_____

Word of the Day

Pain
mental or emotional suffering or torment

The Prayer of Jabez

What or Who has caused you pain.

_____ cried out to the God of Israel, "Oh, that you would bless me and enlarge my_____ _____! Let your hand be with me, and keep me from harm so that I will be free from _____." And God granted his request.

1 Chronicles 4:10 NIV

My Daily Journal

DAY:

Today, I accomplished :

_____
_____
_____
_____

My Goals For Tomorrow:

_____
_____
_____
_____

MyThoughts:

_____
_____
_____
_____

Word of the Day

Why

a question concerning the cause or reason for which something is done, achieved

Why Prayer

"Dear Heavenly Father, please show me my why. Let my why line up to your will and not mine so I can operate strongly in my purpose while on my road to my destiny.
God, speak to me in a voice I can't deny or turn a silent ear to. I pray this prayer in Jesus name. Amen."

My Daily Journal

DAY:

Today, I accomplished :

_____
_____
_____
_____

My Goals For Tomorrow:

_____
_____
_____
_____

MyThoughts:

_____
_____
_____
_____

Word of the Day

Message
a communication containing some information, news, advice, request, or the like, sent by messenger, telephone, email, or other means.

Message Prayer

"Dear Heavenly Father, please show me my message. Let my message line up to your will and not mine so I can operate strongly in my purpose while on the road to my destiny. God speak to me in a voice I can't deny or turn a silent ear too. I pray this prayer in Jesus name. Amen."

My Daily Journal

DAY:

Today, I accomplished :

_____

_____

_____

_____

My Goals For Tomorrow:

_____

_____

_____

_____

MyThoughts:

_____

_____

_____

_____

Word of the Day

Vision
the act or power of anticipating that which will or may come to be

Your Vision Prayer

"Dear Heavenly Father, please give me a vision. Reveal to me my vision and guide me to line up to your will and not mine so I can operate strongly in my vision and purpose ..." You see how vision and purpose has to work together. *"...while on my road to my destiny. God show me my vision so I can't deny or turn a blind eye to it. I pray this prayer in Jesus name. Amen."*

My Daily Journal

DAY:

Today, I accomplished :

_____
_____
_____
_____

My Goals For Tomorrow:

_____
_____
_____
_____

MyThoughts:

_____
_____
_____
_____

Word of the Day

Discouraged
to deprive of courage, hope, or confidence; dishearten; dispirit

Vow Prayer

You are making a vow to God about you and where you are. You are making a vow God to step out and do what you have been called to do and not let your past hurts, your past disappointments discourage you from taking that next step, and then not being afraid to speak your truth.

My Daily Journal

DAY:

Today, I accomplished :

_____
_____
_____
_____

My Goals For Tomorrow:

_____
_____
_____
_____

MyThoughts:

_____
_____
_____
_____

Word of the Day

Expectation

to expect; look forward to; be sure of

What Are Your Expectation?

Don't over think it...just write it down.

My Daily Journal

DAY:

Today, I accomplished :

_____
_____
_____
_____

My Goals For Tomorrow:

_____
_____
_____
_____

MyThoughts:

_____
_____
_____
_____

Word of the Day

Image

an optical counterpart or appearance of an object, as is produced by reflection from a mirror, refraction by a lens, or the passage of luminous rays through a small aperture and their reception on a surface.

Mirror Challenge

What Do You See??

What Do You Want to See??

My Daily Journal

DAY:

Today, I accomplished :

_____

_____

_____

_____

My Goals For Tomorrow:

_____

_____

_____

_____

MyThoughts:

_____

_____

_____

_____

Word of the Day

Armor

any covering worn as a defense against weapons.

Your Armor
What Does Your Armor Look Like?

My Daily Journal

DAY:

Today, I accomplished :

_____
_____
_____
_____
_____

My Goals For Tomorrow:

_____
_____
_____
_____

MyThoughts:

_____
_____
_____
_____

Word of the Day

Winning
the act of a person or thing that wins

Winning
How are you winning?

My Daily Journal

DAY:

Today, I accomplished :

_____
_____
_____
_____

My Goals For Tomorrow:

_____
_____
_____
_____

MyThoughts:

_____
_____
_____
_____

Word of The Day

_____

When Purpose and destiny collide your territory must enlarge!

My Daily Journal

DAY:

Today, I accomplished :

_____
_____
_____
_____

My Goals For Tomorrow:

_____
_____
_____
_____

MyThoughts:

_____
_____
_____
_____

Word of The Day

_____

When Purpose and destiny collide your territory must enlarge!

My Daily Journal

DAY:

Today, I accomplished :

_____
_____
_____
_____

My Goals For Tomorrow:

_____
_____
_____
_____

MyThoughts:

_____
_____
_____
_____

Word of The Day

When Purpose and destiny collide your territory must enlarge!

My Daily Journal

DAY:

Today, I accomplished :

_____
_____
_____
_____

My Goals For Tomorrow:

_____
_____
_____
_____

MyThoughts:

_____
_____
_____
_____

Word of The Day

_____

When Purpose and destiny collide your territory must enlarge!

My Daily Journal

DAY:

Today, I accomplished :

_____
_____
_____
_____

My Goals For Tomorrow:

_____
_____
_____
_____

MyThoughts:

_____
_____
_____
_____

Word of The Day

When Purpose and destiny collide your territory must enlarge!

My Daily Journal

DAY:

Today, I accomplished :

_____
_____
_____
_____

My Goals For Tomorrow:

_____
_____
_____
_____

MyThoughts:

_____
_____
_____
_____

Word of The Day

_____

Word of The Day

_____

When Purpose and destiny collide your territory must enlarge!

My Daily Journal

DAY:

Today, I accomplished :

_____
_____
_____
_____
_____

My Goals For Tomorrow:

_____
_____
_____
_____
_____

MyThoughts:

_____
_____
_____
_____

When Purpose and destiny collide your territory must enlarge!

My Daily Journal

DAY:

Today, I accomplished :

_____
_____
_____
_____

My Goals For Tomorrow:

_____
_____
_____
_____

MyThoughts:

_____
_____
_____
_____

Word of The Day

My Daily Journal

DAY:

Today, I accomplished :

_____
_____
_____
_____

My Goals For Tomorrow:

_____
_____
_____
_____

MyThoughts:

_____
_____
_____
_____

When Purpose and destiny collide your territory must enlarge!

Word of The Day

When Purpose and destiny collide your territory must enlarge!

My Daily Journal

DAY:

Today, I accomplished :

_____
_____
_____
_____

My Goals For Tomorrow:

_____
_____
_____
_____

MyThoughts:

_____
_____
_____
_____

Word of The Day

My Daily Journal

DAY:

Today, I accomplished :

_____
_____
_____
_____

My Goals For Tomorrow:

_____
_____
_____
_____

MyThoughts:

_____
_____
_____
_____

When Purpose and destiny collide your territory must enlarge!

Word of The Day

_____

When Purpose and destiny collide your territory must enlarge!

My Daily Journal

DAY:

Today, I accomplished :

_____

_____

_____

_____

My Goals For Tomorrow:

_____

_____

_____

_____

MyThoughts:

_____

_____

_____

_____

Word of The Day

My Daily Journal

DAY:

Today, I accomplished :

_____

_____

_____

_____

My Goals For Tomorrow:

_____

_____

_____

_____

MyThoughts:

_____

_____

_____

_____

When Purpose and destiny collide your territory must enlarge!

Word of The Day

When Purpose and destiny collide your territory must enlarge!

My Daily Journal

DAY:

Today, I accomplished :

_____
_____
_____
_____
_____

My Goals For Tomorrow:

_____
_____
_____
_____

MyThoughts:

_____
_____
_____
_____

Word of The Day

My Daily Journal

DAY:

Today, I accomplished :

_____
_____
_____
_____

My Goals For Tomorrow:

_____
_____
_____
_____

MyThoughts:

_____
_____
_____
_____

When Purpose and destiny collide your territory must enlarge!

Word of The Day

_____

When Purpose and destiny collide your territory must enlarge!

My Daily Journal

DAY:

Today, I accomplished :

_____
_____
_____
_____

My Goals For Tomorrow:

_____
_____
_____
_____

MyThoughts:

_____
_____
_____
_____

Word of The Day

My Daily Journal

DAY:

Today, I accomplished :

_____
_____
_____
_____

My Goals For Tomorrow:

_____
_____
_____
_____

MyThoughts:

_____
_____
_____
_____

Word of The Day

Word of The Day

When Purpose and destiny collide your territory must enlarge!

My Daily Journal

DAY:

Today, I accomplished :

_____
_____
_____
_____
_____

My Goals For Tomorrow:

_____
_____
_____
_____
_____

MyThoughts:

_____
_____
_____
_____
_____

When Purpose and destiny collide your territory must enlarge!

My Daily Journal

DAY:

Today, I accomplished :

_____
_____
_____
_____

My Goals For Tomorrow:

_____
_____
_____
_____

MyThoughts:

_____
_____
_____
_____

Word of The Day

Word of The Day

_____

When Purpose and destiny collide your territory must enlarge!

My Daily Journal

DAY:

Today, I accomplished :

_____
_____
_____
_____

My Goals For Tomorrow:

_____
_____
_____
_____

MyThoughts:

_____
_____
_____
_____

When Purpose and destiny collide your territory must enlarge!

My Daily Journal

DAY:

Today, I accomplished :

_____
_____
_____
_____

My Goals For Tomorrow:

_____
_____
_____
_____

MyThoughts:

_____
_____
_____
_____